Table of Contents

Map Whiz Quiz

Take a look at the map on page five. Trace the outline of Australia onto a piece of paper. Find the Indian Ocean. Mark this side of your map with a *W* for west. Look for the Coral Sea. Mark this side with an *E* for east. Can you find the island of Tasmania? Colour the water between Tasmania and Australia blue. It is the Bass **Strait**. Colour Australia and Tasmania red to show that they are part of the same country.

Welcome!

Australia is a country that takes up an entire **continent**. Check out the **map** on page five. Two oceans (the Pacific Ocean and the Indian Ocean) and four seas (the Tasman Sea, the Coral Sea, the Timor Sea and the Arafura Sea) touch Australia's shores. Australia's closest neighbour is Papua New Guinea, a small **island** country to the north.

Australia is broken up into six states (Queensland, New South Wales, Victoria, South Australia, Western Australia and Tasmania) and two territories (the Northern Territory and the Australian Capital Territory).

AUSTRALIA

Sean McCollum

Lerner Books • London • New York • Minneapolis

First published in the United Kingdom in 2009 by
Lerner Books,
Dalton House,
60 Windsor Avenue,
London SW19 2RR

Website address: www.lernerbooks.co.uk

This edition was updated and edited for UK publication by Discovery Books Ltd.,
Unit 3, 37 Watling Street, Leintwardine, Shropshire SY7 0LW

Words in **bold** type are explained in the glossary on page 46.

British Library Cataloguing in Publication Data

McCollum, Sean
Australia. - (Country explorers)
1. Australia - Juvenile literature
I. Title
994'.07

ISBN-13: 978 1 58013 485 9

Printed in Singapore

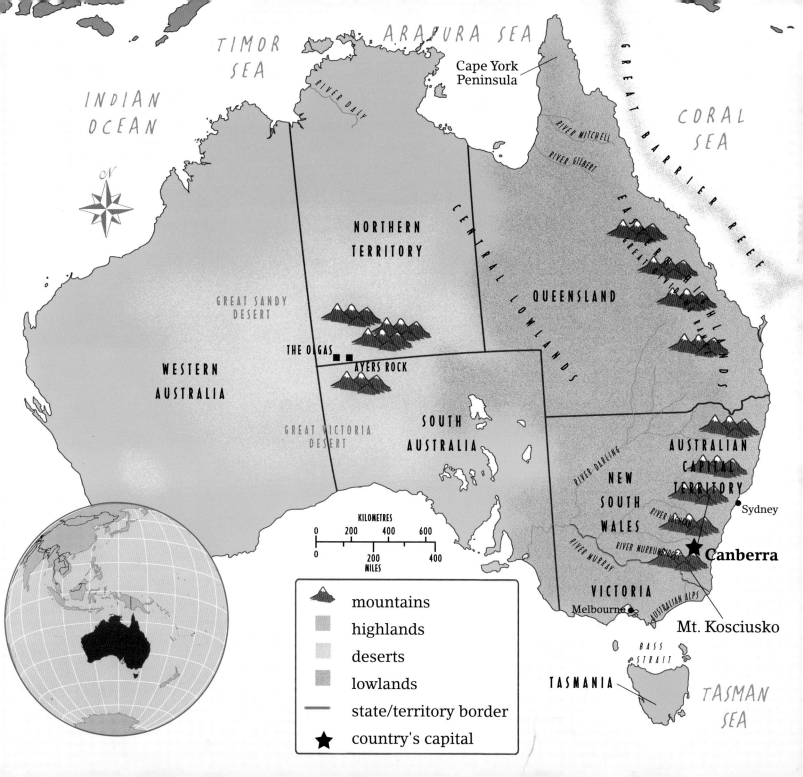

TIMOR SEA

ARAFURA SEA

INDIAN OCEAN

CORAL SEA

GREAT BARRIER REEF

Cape York Peninsula

RIVER DALY

RIVER MITCHELL

RIVER GILBERT

N

CENTRAL LOWLANDS

NORTHERN TERRITORY

QUEENSLAND

EASTERN HIGHLANDS (GREAT DIVIDING HIGHLANDS)

GREAT SANDY DESERT

WESTERN AUSTRALIA

THE OLGAS

AYERS ROCK

GREAT VICTORIA DESERT

SOUTH AUSTRALIA

RIVER DARLING

AUSTRALIAN CAPITAL TERRITORY

NEW SOUTH WALES

RIVER LACHLAN

Sydney

RIVER MURRAY

RIVER MURRUMBIDGEE

★ Canberra

VICTORIA

Melbourne

AUSTRALIAN ALPS

Mt. Kosciusko

BASS STRAIT

TASMANIA

TASMAN SEA

KILOMETRES

0   200   400   600

0   200   400

MILES

mountains

highlands

deserts

lowlands

state/territory border

★ country's capital

Dry and Flat

Do you like to make sand castles? Then Australia is the place for you! Aside from the many beaches, more than half of the country is **desert**. Australians call it the outback. The Great Sandy Desert and the Great Victoria Desert stretch across this area. **Plateaus** cover the rest of the land.

The outback is very dry and dusty. It has some of the hottest weather on Earth.

A set of low **mountains** reaches from the Cape York Peninsula in the north almost to the city of Melbourne in the south. Near the country's southern end is its highest point, Mount Kosciusko.

Australian wine is popular around the world. These vineyards are in New South Wales.

Seasons

Australia lies south of the **equator**. In countries south of the equator, seasons are opposite from those in nations north of the equator.

These boys are having a snowball fight in June.

When it is summer in the north, it is winter in the south. But even winter temperatures in the outback stay around 25°C. In summer, it gets hotter. Daily high temperatures are 38°C! That is HOT!

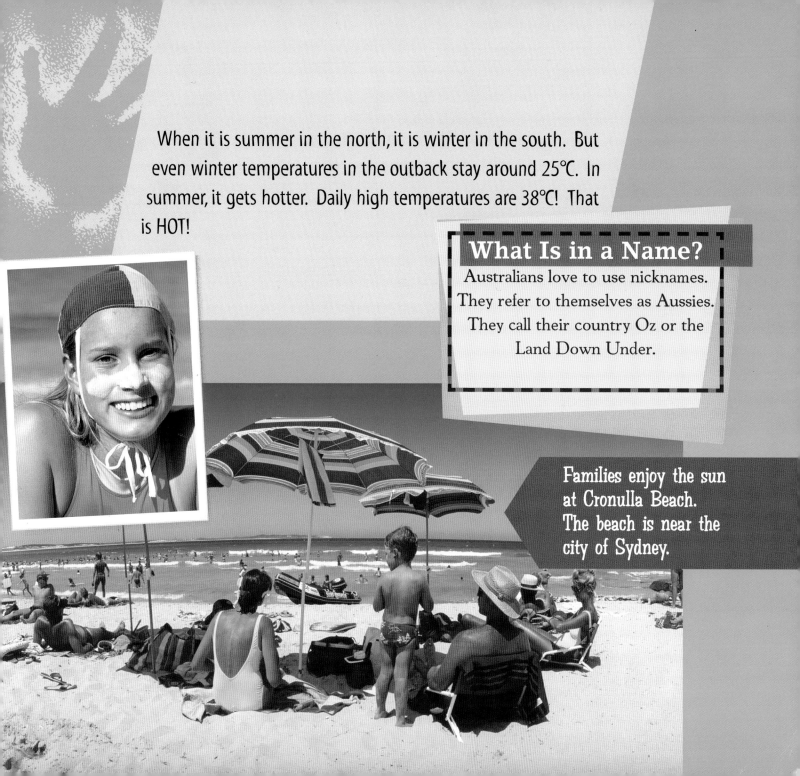

What Is in a Name?

Australians love to use nicknames. They refer to themselves as Aussies. They call their country Oz or the Land Down Under.

Families enjoy the sun at Cronulla Beach. The beach is near the city of Sydney.

Wildlife

Have you ever gone to the zoo? Then you may have seen kangaroos and koalas. Both of these strange animals come from Australia.

Baby koalas ride on their mothers' backs until they are big enough to take care of themselves.

NEXT 15 km

A kangaroo mum carries her baby, called a joey, in a pouch on her belly as she hops around. The koala does not hop, but it also carries its baby in a pouch. Koalas love to eat the leaves of eucalyptus trees.

Sidetrack

About forty different kinds of kangaroos live in Australia. Red kangaroos can hop up to 65 kilometres (40 miles) an hour. And they can jump as high as 6 metres! Boing!

A joey lives in its mother's pouch for about nine months.

11

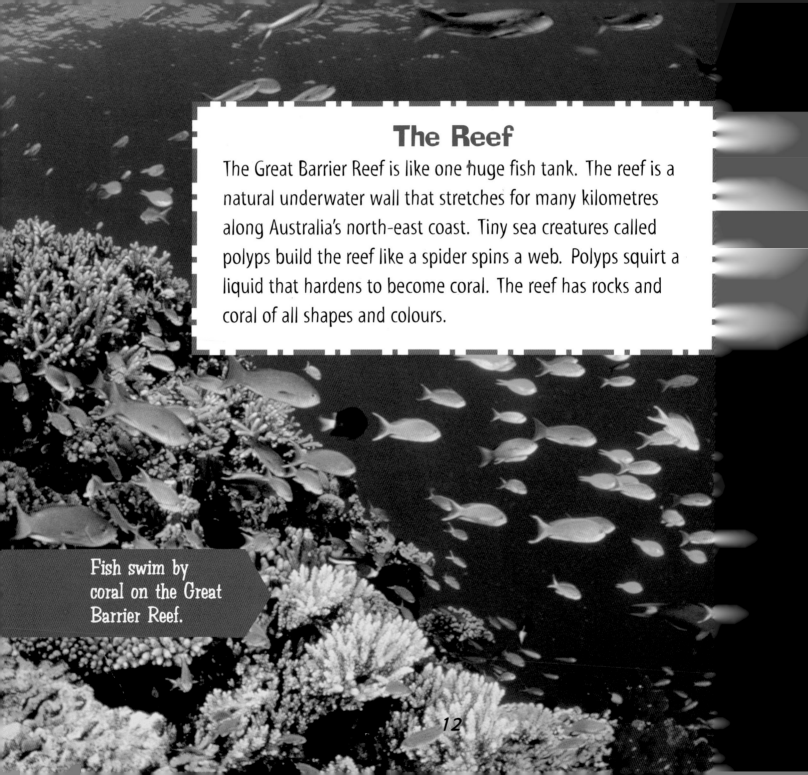

The Reef

The Great Barrier Reef is like one huge fish tank. The reef is a natural underwater wall that stretches for many kilometres along Australia's north-east coast. Tiny sea creatures called polyps build the reef like a spider spins a web. Polyps squirt a liquid that hardens to become coral. The reef has rocks and coral of all shapes and colours.

Fish swim by coral on the Great Barrier Reef.

Dear Grandma and Grandpa,
Australia is so much fun! Yesterday we took a boat to Saint Helena Island. We got to take a tour of an old British prison. It was spooky.

Today we stopped near the Sunshine Coast, a sunny stretch of sand on Australia's eastern shore. The beaches are huge! We swam all day. Tomorrow we are driving to Townsville. Dad says we can take a boat out to the Great Barrier Reef and go snorkelling! Yippee!

See you soon!

Your Friend

Your Town

Anywhere

Australia

Young Aborigines prepare for a festival in Alice Springs. The town is in the centre of Australia.

First People

The first people to live in Australia were the **Aborigines**. Aborigines arrived in Australia thousands of years ago. At one time, as many as four hundred separate Aboriginal groups lived throughout the land. Some stayed in one place and farmed. Others walked around the country looking for food and water.

These days, fewer Aborigines live in Australia. Many live in cities and no longer follow the **traditions** of their **ancestors**.

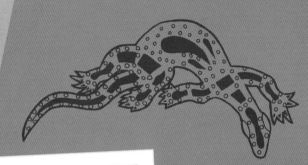

These Aborigine men wear modern, urban clothing.

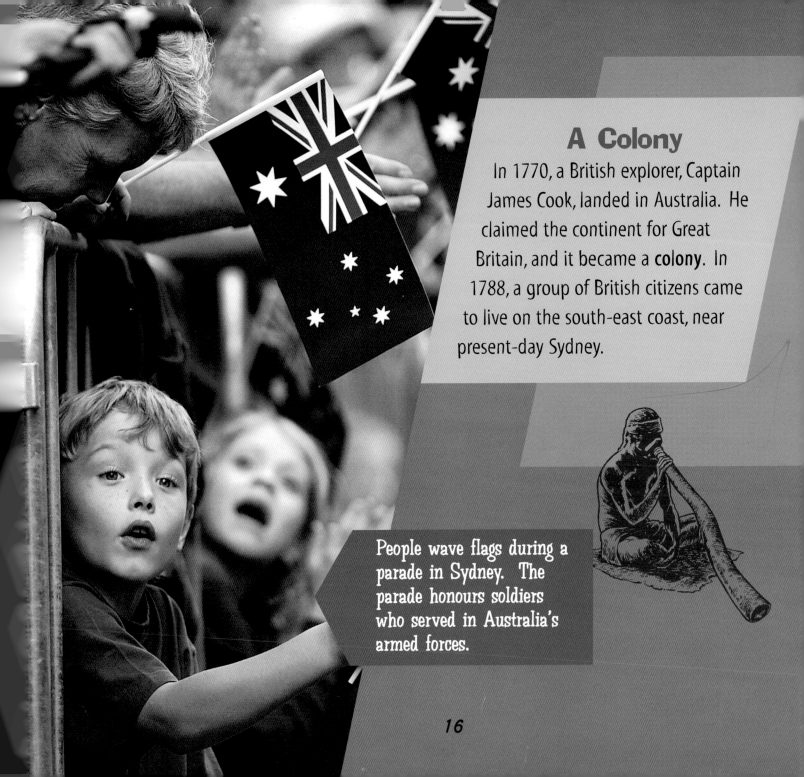

A Colony

In 1770, a British explorer, Captain James Cook, landed in Australia. He claimed the continent for Great Britain, and it became a **colony**. In 1788, a group of British citizens came to live on the south-east coast, near present-day Sydney.

People wave flags during a parade in Sydney. The parade honours soldiers who served in Australia's armed forces.

16

About half of the settlers were prisoners and the others were soldiers the British sent as guards. The prisoners helped build the colony's first farms and homes. Many stayed in Australia after they were freed. Soon other people moved to the colony. Most of them came from Great Britain and Ireland.

Newcomers

These days, Asians are Australia's fastest-growing group of **immigrants**. Many people from China, India, Japan, Vietnam and other Asian countries come in search of better jobs.

Australian children come from all over the world.

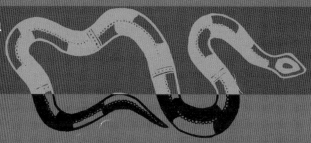

City Life

If you were Australian, you would probably live near a city. Most Australians reside in homes just outside the city in smaller towns, called **suburbs**. Usually Aussie children have small back gardens to play in.

The Sydney Opera House opened in 1973.

The Princess Bridge crosses the River Yarra in the city of Melbourne.

Australia's two biggest cities are Sydney and Melbourne. They are both great places to explore. The Sydney Opera House is quite a sight. Its white, curved roofs look like seashells or like a ship's sails. In Melbourne, you can tour the city on an electric tram. Tram cars are like buses, but they run along city streets on rails like trains. All aboard!

A tram picks up riders at Flinders Street Station in Melbourne.

19

Country Life

Some Aussie children daydream about growing up to be jilleroos or jackaroos. Sometimes they're just called roos. That is what Australians call cowgirls and cowboys. Children think it sounds like fun to ride horseback and round up animals.

This jackaroo herds cows in Dungowan, New South Wales.

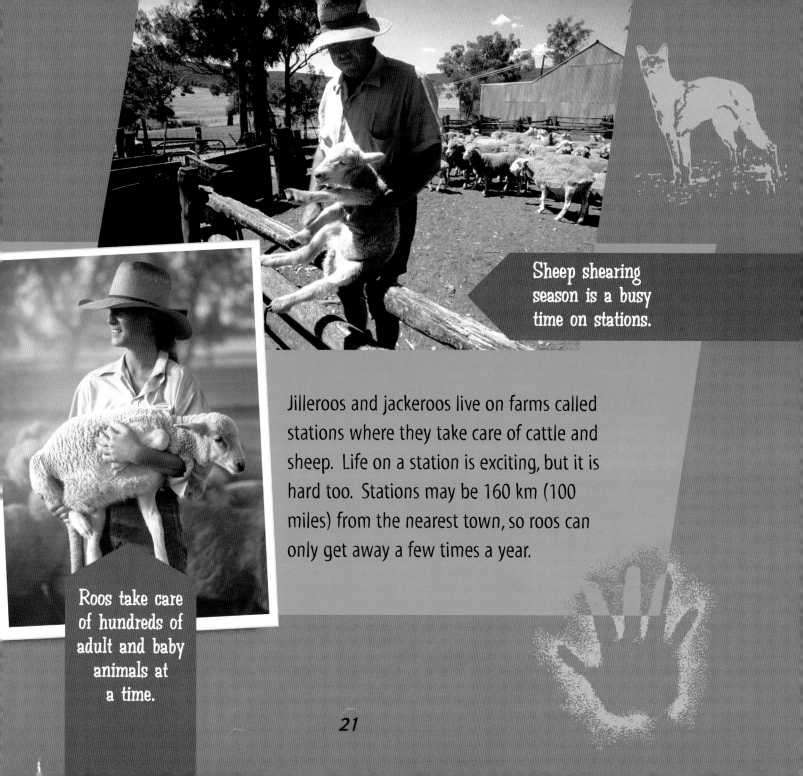

Sheep shearing season is a busy time on stations.

Jilleroos and jackeroos live on farms called stations where they take care of cattle and sheep. Life on a station is exciting, but it is hard too. Stations may be 160 km (100 miles) from the nearest town, so roos can only get away a few times a year.

Roos take care of hundreds of adult and baby animals at a time.

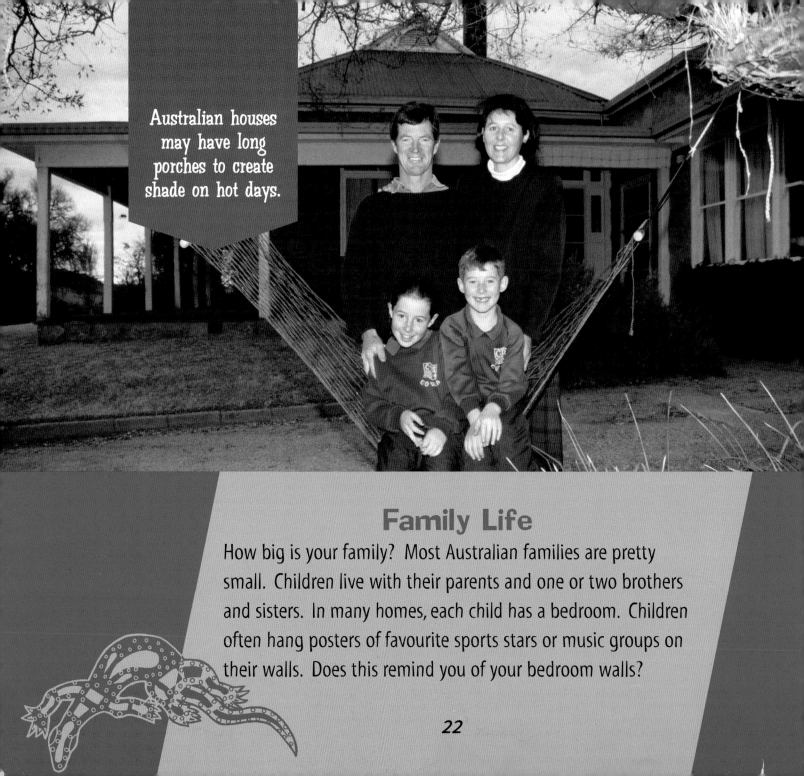

Australian houses may have long porches to create shade on hot days.

Family Life

How big is your family? Most Australian families are pretty small. Children live with their parents and one or two brothers and sisters. In many homes, each child has a bedroom. Children often hang posters of favourite sports stars or music groups on their walls. Does this remind you of your bedroom walls?

When everyone gets home from work or school, families enjoy evenings together. After dinner, parents and children may sit down to watch the telly.

Australian families often eat dinner together. Does your family?

Aussie Talk

Aussies speak English. They picked up a lot of British words and sayings as part of everyday Australian speech. But Australians have their own accent and do not sound at all like the British. Aborigines have their own languages but also speak English.

These men are cheering for their favourite rugby team.

When an Aussie says 'good day,' it sounds like 'g' day.' 'Buy' sounds like 'boy.' Aussies call their form of English 'Strine.' That is short for 'Australian'.

Aussie Speak

Here are a few Strine words and their English meanings.

Aussie	Australian
barbie	barbecue
blue	argument
bonzer	fantastic
chewi	chewing gum
chook	chicken
fair dinkum	really
g' day	good day
sticky beak	nosy person

Friends enjoy a meal off the 'barbie'.

Religion

Most Australians are Christians - usually Protestants or Roman Catholics. Aussies typically do not go to services regularly, but they celebrate marriages, baptisms and funerals at church. A small number of Australians are Buddhists, Hindus, Jews, Muslims or Sikhs.

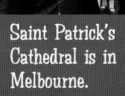

Saint Patrick's Cathedral is in Melbourne.

These men are priests at the Coptic Orthodox Church in Bexley.

Dreamtime

Dreamtime is a set of Aboriginal religious beliefs about the creation of the world. Aborigines believe that powerful spirits moved about the Earth creating mountains, deserts, animals and people. When the spirit creatures were finished, they disappeared. These days, Aborigines pay their respects to the spirits through dances and ceremonies.

This Aboriginal tree bark painting shows figures from the Dreamtime.

Celebrate!

Australians watch fireworks and parades on Australia Day on 26 January. Long ago on that day, the first British settlers arrived to set up the colony. In 1901, Australia won its freedom from Great Britain. Aussies celebrate both events on Australia Day.

Australians also watch fireworks on New Year's Eve in Sydney.

Australians celebrate other festivals too. Christmas, called Chrissie, falls in the middle of Australia's summer. On some Aussie Christmas cards, Santa Claus wears a swimsuit! Aboriginal groups hold corroborees, or festivals, throughout the year. Dancers paint their bodies and act out stories of magic and bravery. These celebrations help Aboriginal leaders teach young Aborigines about their culture.

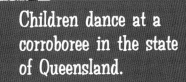

Children dance at a corroboree in the state of Queensland.

Sport

Australians love sport. Rugby and cricket are the most popular. Boys and girls play at every school. Football is also becoming more and more popular in Australia.

Australians play two kinds of rugby - traditional rugby and Australian Rules football. Australian Rules is the Aussies' own brand of rugby. Players kick, run and pass the ball down the field just like in normal rugby, but Australian Rules is faster and rougher.

Australian rugby is rough, tough and very exciting.

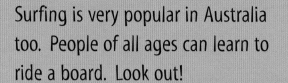

Surfing is very popular in Australia too. People of all ages can learn to ride a board. Look out!

Cricket is very popular in Australia. The Aussie team is one of the best in the world!

Some Aborigines eat grubs and bugs. It is a traditional food from their desert homeland.

Food

When Australians get hungry, they eat tucker. That's the Australian word for 'food'. For breakfast, or 'brekkie', most children eat cereal or toast. Sometimes they have eggs, baked beans or sausages.

On many dinner tables, you will find meat, potatoes and vegetables. Australian immigrants, though, have spiced things up a bit. Greek, Italian and Asian newcomers brought their countries' favourite recipes with them.

A Taste of Australia

Australians love to barbecue on the barbie (not the doll but the grill!). They cook beefburgers, sausages, chicken, prawns and fish. You might be surprised by their favourite burger topping - a slice of beetroot.

This restaurant owner's family is from Greece. He cooks Italian, Greek and Australian meals.

Children at an
Aboriginal school
learn to read.

School Time

Time for school! Classes begin at nine o'clock and end at
three o'clock in the afternoon. Students study reading,
writing, maths, computers and foreign languages, such as
German, French and Japanese.

Children break for a small snack, called morning tea. At twelve thirty, students have an hour to eat a big lunch and to relax.

Schools of the Air

If you lived 100 km (60 miles) from any town, how would you get to school? Australians in the outback go to Schools of the Air. Children use special radios that bring the classroom to them. They listen to and speak to their teacher and classmates, who are also using radios. Many children also use computers to send and receive lessons. One School of the Air calls itself the world's largest classroom. It has kids in an area of 1.3 million sq. km (500,000 square miles)!

Kids use long distance radios to attend Schools of the Air.

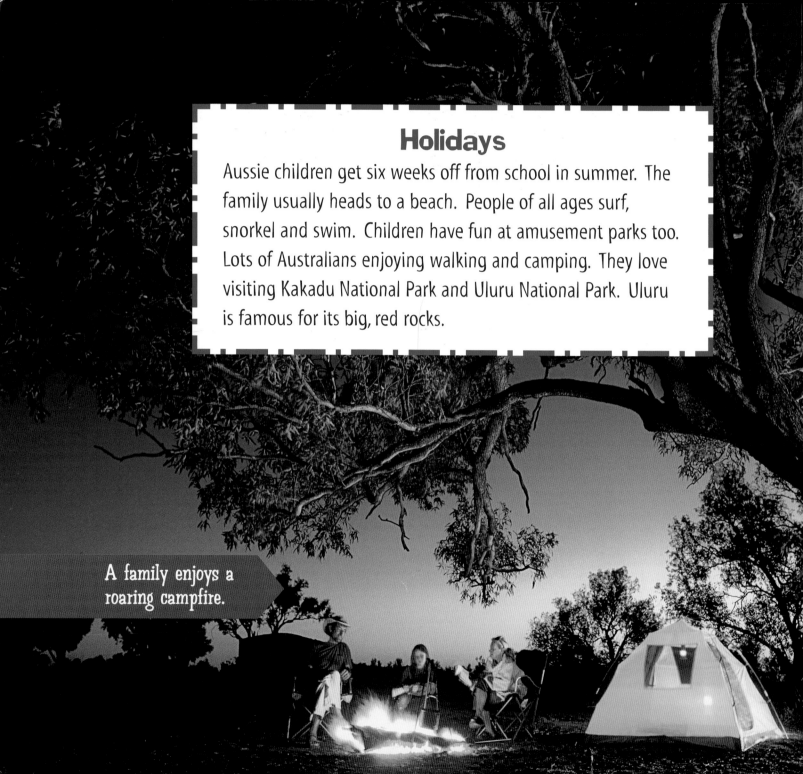

Holidays

Aussie children get six weeks off from school in summer. The family usually heads to a beach. People of all ages surf, snorkel and swim. Children have fun at amusement parks too. Lots of Australians enjoying walking and camping. They love visiting Kakadu National Park and Uluru National Park. Uluru is famous for its big, red rocks.

A family enjoys a roaring campfire.

A tourist enjoys a quiet beach in Queensland.

Ayers Rock

Uluru, also called Ayers Rock, draws many tourists. In fact, Aborigines believe Ayers Rock is where the world began.

Art

Have you ever chalked your name on a pavement? You were leaving behind clues about who you are and where you have been. Aborigines have marked special places all over Australia with paintings and carvings of animals and hunters. Their art tells stories about their history and their beliefs.

Some Aboriginal paintings are almost like maps. This one is done with many tiny dots.

Aborigines tell stories in paintings like this one about Dreamtime.

Aborigines of the outback are famous for the paintings they make with tiny dots. Almost like maps, the paintings point out landmarks or good places to find water. Some Aboriginal art is made up of hundreds of circles. Do not get dizzy!

Crocodiles are hunted for meat. Croc skins are made into shoes and handbags.

Films

The film *Crocodile Dundee* gives us a glimpse of the Australian outback and a taste of Aussie humour. In case you have not seen the film, the main character is a hunter named Crocodile Dundee. (Can you guess what animal he hunts?) Dundee claims that a crocodile bit off one of his legs and that he crawled for a long, long way before he found help.

Throughout the movie, Dundee handles new challenges in ways that make viewers chuckle. Like Dundee, Aussies are known for laughing in the face of danger.

Rock and Roll

Aussies love to make music. Kids on every continent sing along with Aussie rock and pop acts, such as Kylie Minogue, The Vines, Jet, INXS and Keith Urban.

Nicole Kidman is a famous actress from Australia.

What to Read

Australian authors know what kids want to read. Paul Jennings and Morris Gleitzman have many fans. Children laugh at the stories Gleitzman writes, especially *Second Childhood* and *Belly Flop*. Jennings keeps children turning pages in *The Naked Ghost* and *The Gizmo*.

Morris Gleitzman moved to Australia when he was sixteen years old.

Paul Jennings was a teacher before he started writing books.

Making Rivers

Aboriginal stories explain the mysteries of nature. The tale of the Rainbow Serpent, for example, tells how rivers and lakes came to be. By slithering across the ground, the giant snake created rivers. It formed lakes in the spots where it curled up to sleep.

Jennings and Gleitzman worked together on a series of spooky books called *Wicked*. In these books, Dawn and Rory have adventures with the slobberers – worms that can suck out the insides of living things! Yuck!

THE FLAG OF AUSTRALIA

Australia's flag has the British Union Jack in the upper left corner. This part of the flag represents the country's history as a British colony. The large, white star under the Union Jack stands for the country's states and territories. The five white stars on the right side of the flag stand for the constellation called the Southern Cross. It is seen in the Southern Hemisphere, where Australia is located.

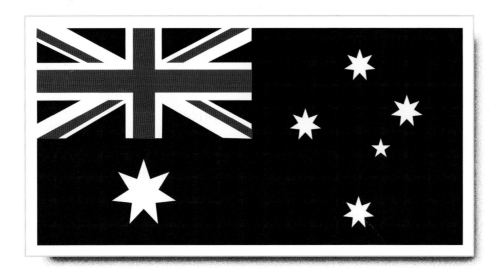

FAST FACTS

FULL COUNTRY NAME: Commonwealth of Australia

AREA: 7,686,849 square kilometres (2,967,909 square miles), including the island of Tasmania. That is roughly the size of western Europe

CAPITAL CITY: Canberra

OFFICIAL LANGUAGE: English

POPULATION: about 20,619,096

SOME MAJOR LANDFORMS:

MOUNTAINS: Great Dividing Range, Australian Alps, Mount Kosciusko, MacDonnell and Musgrave

RIVERS: Alice, Asburton, Atzmay, Daly, Darling, Gascoyne, Gilbert, Lachlan, Mitchell, Murray, Murrumbidgee, Roper, Snowy and Warrego

DESERTS: Gibson, Great Sandy, Great Victoria, Simpson and Tanami

PLATEAUS: Eastern Highlands, Western Plateau

ANIMALS AND THEIR HABITATS:

DESERTS AND GRASSLAND: kangaroos, wallabies

FORESTS: koalas (in eucalyptus trees), kookaburras

RIVERS: platypuses

OCEANS: great white sharks

GLOSSARY

Aborigines: the original people of a land or country; Australia's native peoples

ancestors: relatives who lived long ago

colony: a territory ruled by a country that is far away

continent: any one of seven large areas of land. The continents are Africa, Antarctica, Asia, Australia, Europe, North America and South America.

desert: a dry, sandy region

Dreamtime: a set of Aboriginal religious beliefs about the creation of the world

equator: an imaginary line that circles the Earth around the middle. It divides the world into a north half and a south half

immigrants: people who move from a home country to another country to live

island: a piece of land surrounded by water

map: a drawing or chart showing all or part of the Earth

mountains: parts of the Earth's surface that rise high into the sky

plateaus: large areas of high, level land

strait: a narrow strip of water that connects two larger bodies of water

suburbs: small housing communities that are close to large cities

traditions: ways of doing things – such as preparing a meal, celebrating a festival or making a living – that a group of people have practised for a long time

TO LEARN MORE

BOOKS

Bancroft, Bronwyn. *An Australian ABC of Animals* Little Hare Books, 2005.

Bingham, Jane. *Exploring Australia* (Exploring Continents) Heinemann Library, 2007.

Spilsbury, Richard and Louise Spilsbury. *Watching Kangaroos in Australia* (First Library: Wild World) Heinemann Library, 2006.

Thompson, Ruth and David Hampton. *Australia* (Living in) Franklin Watts Ltd., 2005.

WEBSITES

Australia-Kids Down Under
http://www.gigglepotz.com/caustralia.htm
Visit this site for a wealth of information about Australia, and learn what it's like to be a child Down Under. Find out about Australian animals, famous people, special holidays and more. You can even print an Aussie map and flag.

Seven Wonders of the World
http://library.thinkquest.org/J002388/ayersrock.html
See photos and learn more about Ayers Rock and the Great Barrier Reef.

INDEX

The photographs in this book are reproduced with the permission of: © Ian Waldie/Getty Images, p 6; © Ryan Pierse/Getty Images, p 8; © Matt Turner/ Getty Images, p 14; © Nick Wilson/Getty Images, p 16; © Jonathan Wood/Getty Images, p 30; Australian Tourist Commission, pp 7, 9 (both), 10 (right), 13, 18 (upper right), 21 (left), 29; © Tim Graham Photo Library/Getty Images, p 10 (left); © John W. Banagan/Stone/Getty Images, p 11; © Gary Bell/Taxi/Getty Images, p 12; © Reuters/CORBIS, pp 15, 31 (both); © Robin Smith/Art Directors, pp 17, 25, 35; © David Noton/Photographer's Choice/Getty Images, p 18 (bottom); © Anthony Cassidy/Stone/Getty Images, p 19; © Jochen Schlenker/Robert Harding World Imagery/Getty Images, p 20; © Helene Rogers/Art Directors, p 21 (top); © Trip/Art Directors, pp 22, 23; © Matthew King/Getty Images Sport/Getty Images, p 24; © Michael Rayner/Fairfaxphotos, p 26 (left); © Ben Rushton/Fairfaxphotos, p 26 (right); © Penny Tweedie/CORBIS, pp 27, 39; © Robin Smith/Stone/Getty Images, p 28; © Jason Edwards/National Geographic/Getty Images, p 32; © Dieter Telemans/Panos Pictures, p 33; © Bill Bachman, p 34; © David Trood/The Image Bank/Getty Images, p 36; © Panoramic Images/Getty Images, p 37 (top); © John Kreul/Independent Picture Service, p 37 (bottom); © Michele Burgess/SuperStock, p 38; © Davis Factor/CORBIS, p 40; © Alberto Pizzoli/AFP/Getty Images, p 41; © Tim de Neef/Penguin Group (Australia), p 42; Penguin Group (Australia), p 43. Illustrations by © Bill Hauser/Independent Picture Service. Cover: © Free Agents Limited/CORBIS.

First published in the United States of America in 2008.

Text copyright © 2008 by Lerner Publishing Group, Inc.